Ezio Renda

ALL VERONA

115 colour plates

city map featuring major monuments

BET
BONECHI EDIZIONI "IL TURISMO" FIRENZE

Exclusive distributor for Verona:
Randazzo G. Snc. di Randazzo E. e R.
Via Emilei, 22 - 37121 VERONA
Tel. +39-045.800.40.40 - Fax +39-045.803.60.63

© Copyright 1999 by Bonechi Edizioni "Il Turismo" S.r.l
Via dei Rustici, 5 - 50122 FLORENCE
Tel. +39-055.239.82.24/25 - Fax +39-055.21.63.66
E-mail address: barbara@bonechi.com
                    bbonechi@dada.it
http://www.bonechi.com
Printed in Italy

Photos: Bonechi Edizioni "Il Turismo" S.r.l. Archives;
page 63: Stefano Signorini; page 54: per concessione del
Ministero dell'Ambiente e del Patrimonio Culturale -
"Soprintendenza SBAS del Veneto"; Nicola Grifoni; I-Buga
- Milan.
Front cover photographs: from the photo archives of
Randazzo, Verona
Layout: Nina Peci
Photolithography: Bluprint Srl., Florence
Print: BO.BA.DO.MA, Florence
ISBN 88-7204-410-3

Introduction

It could be said that man and nature have combined to make of this city a genuine masterpiece of gracefulness, beauty and harmony. Man's contribution lies in its buildings and works of art, which belong to many different epochs and styles, but which are so closely blended into the fibre of the city that they create a unique effect of unity and continuity. For her part, nature has contributed the pleasant hills around Verona, as well as the majestic river which winds solemnly by, smiling on the city through which it passes. Verona is a city in which the most diverse styles succeed in finding a happy coexistence, where the Gothic church stands next to the Romanesque house, the medieval tower alongside the neoclassical building, the homes of the people beside the homes of the aristocracy. Over the centuries, the slow passage of time has given the city a uniform, scarcely visible patina, so that its stones all have the same pale colouring, a restrained, monochrome tone, which is nonetheless capable of assuming the most delicate shades at different hours of the day or when the wind from the mountains brings a change of weather. Verona is thus a city which derives its vitality from almost imperceptible but subtly evocative moods and emotions.

Fully to experience that sense of magic and romance which the city can offer him, the visitor must walk through it, lose himself in its ancient, narrow streets, and pass his hand over its stones, wet with the dampness of ages. He must open the rusty, creaking iron gates and enter its hidden gardens, push open the doors of its anonymous, lesser known old churches, and disturb the calm of its ancient buildings and silent cloisters. Frequently a casual "glance through a halfopen gate or between tall and picturesque walls will be rewarded by an unexpected glimpse of the shimmering waters of the Adige, in which the city's churches, buildings and towers are reflected. The visitor who sees Verona in this way will immediately understand why so many famous writers have chosen it as the setting for their works. He will feel the force of the intense emotions which Shakespeare infused into his two famous characters, Romeo and Juliet, bringing them to life as the symbol of a perfect and immortal love on the richly evocative stage of Verona. And Verona may seem to him a sort of haven to be reached in man's restless existence, offering the traveller a moment's pause for breath, a sense of peace among the profound silence of its age-old buildings and artifacts, and a sense of the human warmth and life so rarely found in the frenzy of the present day.

View of the fountain in Piazza Bra.

Piazza Erbe

Piazza Erbe (the "Square of the Herbs", so called because at one time only green vegetables were sold here) is one of the most picturesque city squares in the whole of Italy and certainly the most famous in Verona. Sheltered by their white umbrellas, the stalls in the square display the most varied types of merchandise, including fruit and clothing, old gramaphone records which can no longer to be found elsewhere and postcards for the tourists. The square is irregular in form and around it are buildings in different styles and colours. On the left-hand side is the Romanesque building of the **"Domus mercatorum"**, now the headquarters of the Chamber of Commerce, built by Alberto I della Scala in 1301. At the end of the square is the imposing **Palazzo Maffei**, rightly considered Verona's Baroque masterpiece; built in 1688, it is crowned by a loggia with six statues representing *Hercules, Jupiter, Venus, Mercury, Apollo* and *Minerva*. Beside this building is the **Gardello Tower**, begun under Cansignorio della Scala in 1370 and completed in 1626 with the addition of its bell-shaped covering. On the right-hand side is **Casa Mazzanti**, in which are 16th century frescoes of mythological subjects, painted by the artist Alberto Cavalli. On the same side is another **tower**, the **Lamberti Tower** begun in 1172 and 272 feet high. Above the white tops of the umbrellas can be seen the *column* with the *Lion of St. Mark* on top; the *fountain of "Madonna Verona"*, constructed under Cansignorio in 1368; the so-called **"Berlina"**, a small marble loggia dating from the 16th century; and finally a Gothic *tabernac*le with elegant cuspidate decoration.

Bird's-eye view of Piazza Erbe with its lively and colourful stalls and the Gardello Tower at the far end of the square.

Palazzo Maffei with the Column of the Lion of St. Mark and the Fountain of Madonna Verona.

Below:
detail of the Fountain of Madonna Verona and the so-called Berlina, a 15th-century shrine.

Piazza dei Signori with its
monument to Dante
Alighieri.

Below:
the Arch of the Rib;
the statue of Girolamo
Fracastoro with details
of the exquisite decoration
on the Loggia del
Consiglio, a Renaissance
work attributed to Friar
Giocondo.

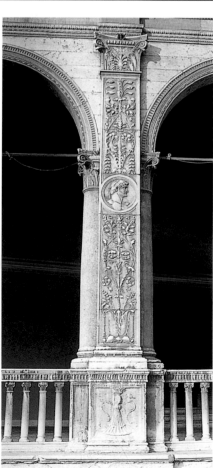

Piazza dei Signori

Whereas the nearby Piazza Erbe is full of irregular shapes and forms, a sort of product of untrammelled architectural fantasy, and is dominated by the popular spirit, Piazza dei Signori is far more rationally planned and pervaded by an aristocratic atmosphere. The buildings around the square are united by graceful arcades, above which are the statues of eminent citizens of Verona, such as *Scipione Maffei* and *Girolamo Fracastoro*. A monument with *Dante's statue*, done by Ugo Zannoni in 1865, stands in the centre of the square, as if to serve as a perpetual reminder to tourists and Veronese alike of the poet's period in exile as a guest of Bartolomeo I della Scala. Immediately noticeable are the two colours on the façade of the **Palazzo del Comune** and the doorway (made by Sanmicheli) of the **Palazzo del Capitano**, in the courtyard of which is the door called the *"Porta Bombardiera"*, dating from 1687. At the end of the square is the **Palazzo degli Scaligeri**, originally a 13th century building but considerably reconstructed in later periods. In its courtyard is a fine Renaissance *well* and a *loggia* with traces of frescoes by Altichiero.

Loggia del Consiglio

This Renaissance-style structure, built between 1476 and 1793, is without doubt the most elegant and distinctive of all the buildings in the square. It is also called the Loggia di Fra' Giocondo, because its design is traditionally attributed to a Veronese monk of that name, though many critics believe rather that it is the work of the Panteo family and their workshop. The design of the loggia is of Tuscan derivation, with mullioned windows above its large double arcades, but the colour is more typical of northern Italy and in particular of Verona itself. The statues above the cornice were sculpted by Alberto da Milano, and represent *Catullus, Pliny, Macer, Vitruvius* and *Cornelius Nepos*, great Veronese of the Roman era.

The elegant Loggia del Consiglio, also called *"Loggia di Frà Giocondo"*.

The Gothic stairway in the Mercato Vecchio (Old Market) courtyard; detail of the courtyard in the Palazzo degli Scaligeri.

Below:
The richly-imaginative Porta Bombardiera, with its military symbols, in the courtyard of the Palazzo.

Courtyard of the Mercato Vecchio

This is the courtyard inside the Palazzo del Comune; it is quadrangular in plan, and its powerful Romanesque structure is lightened by the typical Veronese use of alternating bands of stone and bricks, giving a two-colour effect. Chiaroscuro contrasts also derive from the portico on the lower floor, with its pillars and wide arches, and the elegant Gothic stairway with two ramps of stairs, called the "Stairway of Reason", built between 1446 and 1450. The three-mullioned windows over the archways also interrupt the solidity of the walls and introduce yet another pictoric effect.

Scaliger Tombs

Inside a marble enclosure, protected by an iron fence reproducing the motif of the ladder (the meaning of "scala" and the symbol of the family), are the funeral monuments of the Scala family, rulers of Verona from 1260 to 1387. Each lord is represented by two statues on his tomb: one lying on the sarcophagus in the immobility of death, and the other astride his horse on the pinnacle above the monument, wearing his armour as if prepared for yet another battle. The *tomb of Mastino II*, near the entrance, with four *angels* around the sarcophagus, was erected between 1340 and 1350. Many of the other tombs are simple sarcophagi at ground level, such as that of *Giovanni della Scala*, sculpted by a Venetian artist called Andriolo de' Santi.

The Tomb of Mastino II near Santa Maria Antica.

Tomb of Cansignorio

Standing like a huge but delicate piece of lacework, this is the finest of the Scaliger tombs, containing the remains of Cansignorio, who died in 1375. It is the work of Bonino da Campione and Gaspare Broaspini, whose ability as stonemasons was so great that they seem to have handled the unyielding marble as if it were lace. The architectural design of this tomb is the same as that of ten others, but it is enriched by pinnacles and spires, by ornaments and carving both on the base and on the baldachin.

The Tomb of Cansignorio by Bonino da Campione and Gaspare Broaspini.

Previous page:
The Tomb of Cangrande I della Scala, masterpiece of 14th- century Veronese sculpture.

Tomb of Cangrande

The tomb of the Veronese ruler Cangrande I della Scala, who was born in 1291 and died in 1329, stands outside the enclosure which contains the other Scaliger tombs, beside the entrance doorway to the church of Santa Maria Antica, the origins of which date back to the 7th century. Justly considered the masterpiece of Veronese sculpture in the 14th century, the tomb consists of a large Gothic baldachin supported by columns and surmounted by a pyramid, on the top of which is the equestrian statue of Cangrande, a work by a 14th century stone mason known as the "Master of the Scaliger Tombs". The ruler lies under the baldachin in a sarcophagus on which are sculpted an *Annunciation* and a *Pietà*.

Romeo's House

This splendid 14th century dwelling in Via delle Arche Scaligere is held by tradition to be that of the Montecchi, or Montagues, the family to which Romeo belonged. The building, which is unfortunately in a poor state of preservation, is one of the oldest in Verona.

The Montague House, or Romeo's House.

Juliet's House.

Below:
Juliet's legendary balcony.

Juliet's House

Only a few paces from Piazza Erbe is this building, at number 27, Via Cappello, once owned by the Dal Cappello, or Capulet, family. Again according to the legend, this was the house where the beautiful Juliet, the most famous of all Shakespeare's heroines, lived. It probably dates back to the 13th century, and has a brick façade with large trilobate windows. A small marble balcony records the most famous verses of Shakespeare's tragedy, in which Romeo declares his love for Juliet as she stands on the balcony.

The Borsari Gate and the
"Wing" of the Arena, with
the Shrine of the Virgin.

Below:
the entrance courtyard to
the Maffeiano Stonework
Museum and the
Gateways (Portoni)
to the Bra.

Porta Borsari

Constructed at the end of the 1st century A.D. and restored in 265 under the Emperor Gallien, the gate derives its name from the "borsarii", the Roman excise-men who collected payments on the goods at the various entrances to the city. This was the *decuman* gate, through which the most important road in the Roman network entered the city. The gate was part of the first circle of city walls, and still has its two barrel vaults with columns, architraves and tympanums, above which is a double order of windows, twelve in all. On the architrave can still be seen the inscription of the name given to the city under Roman rule: COLONIA AUGUSTA VERONA.

Piazza Bra

This large, open square, full of light, is a splendid amalgam of various different styles. One enters the square beneath the double archway called the *"Portoni"*, part of a battlemented wall built under Gian Galeazzo Visconti, alongside the **Pentagon Tower**, dating from 1389. The centre of the square is occupied by a fine garden, in the middle of which is a fountain and two monuments from more recent times. The Bra is a square of irregular shape, around which stand the **Palazzo della Gran Guardia**, built in 1610 by Domenico Curtoni in a style clearly influenced by Sanmicheli; the **Palazzo Barbieri**, headquarters of the *municipal government*, a building in neoclassical style erected in 1838 by G. Barbieri; and at number 16 the **Palazzo Guastaverza**, a work by Sanmicheli dating from 1555. But the Bra would not be so well known were it not for its celebrated **Listone**, the wide footpath which follows the curving line of the buildings around the square. This is perhaps the favourite meeting-place of the Veronese people, where they most frequently come together to talk or to take a stroll. Along it are famous cafes, excellent restaurants and elegant shops. In a way, it expresses the gay, open nature of the Veronese themselves, who as they stroll up and down here seem almost to recreate the light and frivolous atmosphere of the 18th century.

Piazza Bra, a splendid mixture of different styles with its lushly verdant gardens; it is the most popular meeting-place of the Veronese.

Arena

Roman Amphitheatre

Erected at the beginning of the 1st century A.D., the amphitheatre is now best known as the Arena. Originally it was constructed outside the circle of city walls, but for defence purposes it was included in the area within the walls by Gallien in the 3rd century. Only the Colosseum in Rome exceeds the Arena in size and grandeur: it has an elliptical plan, and is 455 feet long and 360 feet wide, while the Arena inside measures 242 feet by 146 feet. Seen from outside, it has two orders of 72 arches made from brick and pink Veronese stone, which create an extremely colourful effect. Originally it had two external walls which have been lost as the result of earthquakes and other destruction: only a magnificent fragment, called by the Veronese the *Ala* or "*Wing*", has remained. Like all the other Roman amphitheatres, the Arena was used for contests between gladiators, games and hunts, which in later centuries gave place to chivalric tournaments, duels and similar spectacles. Later it came to be adopted for theatrical perfomances, and even the great Italian actress Eleonora Duse acted here, in the part of Juliet. Since 1913, the Arena has been the scene of regular seasons of lyric opera, permitting the use of magnificent stage sets in grandiose performances which can be seen by no less than 25,000 spectators (the total capacity of the amphitheatre). These spectacles have been made possible by the continued interest and dedication of the Veronese people to the preservation of what is without doubt their most famous monument. As early as 1580 a special group of administrators, the "*Conservatores Arenae*", was appointed to take charge of the amphitheatre, supervising restoration work when necessary. The first impression which one has on seeing the inside of the Arena is one of great strength, carefully controlled. There is a large stone plinth at the base of the seating area, which is reinforced by 73 brick structures radiating out from the centre.

The fountain in Piazza Bra;
Palazzo Barbieri and the
Palazzo of the Gran Guardia.

The "Wing"
of the Arena.

Below:
The Promenade and
the Arena near via
Mazzini and a detail
of the "Wing".

*On the following
pages:*
grand views
of the Arena.

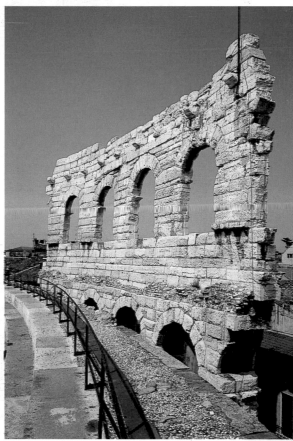

The Arena from the inside.

Below:
the Arena during an opera performance.

Previous page
from the top:
bird's-eye view and the Arena from the inside.

Palazzo Bevilacqua by Michele Sanmicheli.

Next page:
the elegant Gavi Arch, once astride the main road and next to the Castelvecchio Clocktower.

Palazzo Bevilacqua

Palazzo Bevilacqua, at number 19, Via Cavour, was designed by Michele Sanmicheli, and perhaps represents only part of a considerably more grandiose project, as is suggested by the position of the entrance door, towards the left of the façade. According to the art historian Vasari, Sanmicheli was given the commission for the building by Bishop Ludovico of Canossa in about 1530. The pictorial element is predominant in the architecture of Sanmicheli. The second floor of the building is broken up into a sort of rhythmic unity by the alternation of large and small windows and by the original fluting of the columns, emphasising the pictorial element of the loggia. The design of the ground floor is somewhat analogous: the horizontal division created by the rustic ashlar stone is interrupted by the large, decisive windows between the pillars.

Gavi Arch

The arch was built to a design by the architect Lucius Vitruyius Cerdo, commissioned by the Gavi, a Veronese family, in the middle of the 1st century A.D. Square, elegant and slender in form, it was originally situated in the centre of the road leading to the Castelvecchio. In the 18th century it was destroyed by the French, and it was brought here and reconstructed in 1933.

The entrance to Castelvecchio.

Previous page from the top: Crucifixion together with the Virgin and St. John the Evangelist from the Church of San Giacomo di Tomba by the Master of Cellore, and the Tomb of Saints Sergius and Bacchus.

Castelvecchio

The massive and crenellated Castelvecchio (Old Castle), formerly known as the Castello di San Martino, was built as a stronghold by Cangrande II della Scala during the years 1354-55. Incorporated in its structure was an extensive portion of the city walls, terminating at the River Adige. The castle has had a fairly eventful history as it has survived, though not unscathed, successive dominations by various ruling families, plus the Venetians, French and Austrians. The small fort in the inner courtyard was built by Napoleon. For obvious military reasons the castle battlements and towers were cut down, not to be restored until the 1930s, when the ancient fortress was given a new role as a museum. The irregular line of the external walls is punctuated by six roofed towers, one of which, taller and more strongly fortified than the others, is known as the **Mastio** (keep). The castle walls are bounded by a deep moat through which flowed the so-called "Adigetto" (or little Adige). The interior is divided by partition walls which separate it into three courtyards of varying sizes. Recent excavation has unearthed some interesting remains of the castle as it originally was, such as the **Morbio Postern Gate**, part of the inner ramparts, and the remains of the tiny and ancient **church of San Martino**. The fort built by Napoleon underwent considerable changes between 1923 and 1926.

Castelvecchio Museum

The Castelvecchio has been almost fully restored to its original form, thanks to restoration work begun in 1957, under the guidance of C. Scarpa and L. Magagnato. The museum it houses is now considered one of the best laid-out museums in the whole of Europe. The entrance to the museum is on the ground floor, with the offices and library.

Room 1 - Romanesque sculpture influenced by the Veronese style. *Sarcophagus of Saints Sergius* and *Bacchus* (1179), 13th cent. *male figure* attributed to Brioloto and a 12th cent. ciborium in the shape of *female figures supporting a stone slab.*
The modern alcove in the annex houses a precious collection of Longobard jewellery, gold and bronze objects and late Medieval glass.

Room 2 - 14th cent. Veronese sculpture, with statues of *Saints Catherine, Cecilia, John the Baptist* and *Martha*, from the church of San Giacomo di Tomba.

Room 3 - 14th cent. Veronese sculpture, including *Madonna Enthroned, Crucifixion, Madonna, St. Libera.*

Room 4 - Late 14th cent. Veronese sculpture- of note the expressive *Crucifixion* from San Giacomo di Tomba and *Mary and Martha* by the Master of Cellore.

Room 5 - Early 15th cent. sculpture, including *panels with Prophets, St. Martin* (1436) and *St. Peter enthroned.*
The *Morbio Postern Gate* leads to the Great Tower and to the other rooms.

Room 6 - (On the other side of the wall) ancient *bells of Verona*, 14th-18th cents.

Room 7 - (On the first floor) The Da Prato Collection of ancient firearms. This section of the Castle is known as the Royal Palace and is the best preserved.

Room 8 - 13th and 14th cent. frescoes from churches and palaces in Verona.
A glass case contains 14th cent. jewellery of great beauty.

Room 9 - Detached 14th cent. frescoes - *Madonna and Child, the Coronation of the Virgin, Crucifixion* and others.

Saint Cecilia, XIVth Cent. and the Madonna of the Goldfinch by Liberale da Verona.

Below:
Madonna of the Milk by Tintoretto.

Room 10 - *Polyptych of the Trinity* and other works by Turone, an anonymous 14th cent. altar front with *The Seven Saints, Saints and a Nun*, by Tommaso da Modena, and the *Boi Polyptych* by the school of Altichiero.

Room 11 - Examples of the International Gothic School. This is one of the most important collections in the museum, with works by the chief exponents of the late Gothic style. The *Madonna of Humility, St. Jerome, the Resurrection*, all by Jacopo Bellini; the *Madonna of the Quail* by Pisanello, the *Madonna of the Milk* by M. Giambono, the *Madonna of the Rose Garden and a Madonna and Child* by Stefano da Verona. There are also works by Niccolò di Pietro Gerini, Francesco de' Franceschi and a number of miniatures.

Room 12 - Dedicated to the work of foreign artists, among them Jacques Daret, Joachim Patinier, Antonio Moro, Martin Van Cleef, Jean Mostaert Konrad Faber, Giacomo Jordaens, Peter Lely, Peter Paul Rubens, etc.

Room 13 - 14th and 15th cent. paintings, including the *Death of the Virgin* by Giambono, a *Crucifixion* by Jacopo Bellini; the *Aquila*

Polyptych, the *Fracanzani Ancona Resurrection Altarpiece* and many other paintings by Giovanni Badile.

In addition, there is a great *Crucifix*, by the "Master of the Carnation" and a fresco by followers of Altichiero.

Room 14 - (On the top floor of the Royal Palace) Paintings by Veronese artists of the Rennaissance, including Liberale, Nicolò Giolfino, F. Verla, G. Moceto, Domenico Morone, and Giovanni Maria Falconetto.

Room 15 - Venetian masters of the Renaissance period, including Giovanni Bellini, with two paintings of the *Madonna and Child*, Gentile Bellini's *Crucifix of Albarelli*, Vittorio Carpaccio's *Two Saints with a Page*, and works by M. Basaiti, G. Mansueti, and B. Montagna.

Room 16 - Important works by Veronese Renaissance painters, namely Domenico and Francesco Morone and Francesco dai Libri.

Room 17 - Paintings by Francesco Buonsignori, *Allegory of Music*, the *Dal Bovo Madonna* and *Madonna in Adoration*, as well as works by A. Vivarini and G. F. Caroto.

Madonna of the Rose-garden by Stefano da Verona.

Previous page: equestrian statue of Cangrande I della Scala on view inside the Museum.

Deposition by Paolo
Veronese.

Below:
Holy Family and a Saint by
Andrea Mantegna.

Next page from the top:
Boy with a childish
drawing by Giovanni
Francesco Caroto and a
sketch by Tiepolo for the
ceiling of Cà Rezzonico.

Below:
Madonna of the Quail
by Pisanello.

Room 18 - Dedicated primarily to Liberale da Verona, this room houses his *Adoration of the Shepherds*, the *Sambonifacio Dowry Chest*, the *Madonna of the Goldfinch*, and a *Nativity*.

Room 19 - Paintings by Andrea Mantegna: *Christ Carrying the Cross*, *The Holy Family*, *Madonna and Child* with *St. Juliana*. Also here are a *Madonna* by C. Crivelli, a *Holy Conversation* by F. Francia and works by Girolamo dai Libri, F. Benaglio and J. da Valenza.

Room 20 - (Next to the Mastio) Arms and fabrics from the tomb of Cangrande I at Santa Maria Antica. A passageway leads back into the main museum building, past the concrete plinth with the original of the *Statue of Cangrande I on his horse*, from the cemetery of the Scala Family.

Room 21 - *Polyptych* and *Four Saints* by F. Cavazzola, and other works by the same artist. The room also holds *Madonna and Saints* by G. F. Caroto, *Madonna Caliari* by N. Giolfino, and finally, two panels, *A Young Monk* and *Child with a Drawing*, by Caroto.

Room 22 - Chiefly devoted to works by Giovanni Francesco Caroto and Girolamo dai Libri, with his *Madonna Maffei*.

Room 23 - Works of the great 16th cent. Venetian artists: *Deposition, Bevilacqua Altarpiece,* and *Portrait of Pase Guarienti,* by P. Veronese. *Nativity, Madonna of the Milk,* and *Concert of the Muses* by J. Tintoretto. *St. Dorothy* by S. del Piombo and paintings by L. Lotto and B. de' Pitati.

Room 24 - 16th and 17th cent. Veneto artists, especially Jacopo and Francesco Bassano, Paolo Farinati, Felice Brusasorci, F. Maffei, and P. Ottino. Outstanding is the splendid *Woman Taken in Adultery* by Caravaggio's Neapolitan pupil Bernardo Cavallino.

Room 25 - Interesting paintings by Veronese and 17th cent. Venetian artists: M. Bassetti, B. Strozzi and others.

Room 26 - 17th and 18th cent. Venetian art. Works by B. Strozzi, A. Balestra, G. Carpioni, G. Cignaroli, and D. Feti, *Three Carmelite Monks* and *St. Theresa,* and *Sketch for the Ceiling of the Ca' Rezzonico,* by G.B.Tiepolo and also two *Capricci* by F. Guardi.

Note - *The rooms of the Castelvecchio Museum are named after distinguished families or individual citizens of Verona, but these names have not been included in this guide.*

Internal view of the Church of San Lorenzo.

Next page:
two views of the Ponte Scaligero (Scaliger Bridge) on the River Adige.

San Lorenzo

A masterpiece of Verona's Romanesque style, it stands on the site of a former Early Christian church, decorative fragments of which can still be seen in the entrance courtyard. Its construction dates back to about 1117, but it was partly rebuilt in succeeding eras. Immediately noticeable from the outside are the typical alternating bands of stone and brick and the original architectural motif, of Norman derivation, of the two cylindrical towers which lead to the women's galleries. Inside the church, one is struck at once by the rigorous structural emphasis of its design. The solemnity of the Romanesque style, seen in the rhythmic order of cruciform pillars alternated with double arches and supporting the women's galleries, is subtly and skilfully moderated by the play of colour in the dark and tight bands along the walls, creating a somewhat mystical atmosphere. The church has three naves and three apses, with an altar-piece by Domenico Brusasorci, depicting the *Madonna with Saints*, in the main apse.

Scaliger Bridge

Along with the construction of the Castelvecchio, Cangrande II ordered that a bridge be built, both to link the castle with the other bank of the river and to serve as an escape route from the city. The identity of the builder of this solid, but at the same time graceful, bridge is not known with certainty, though it is thought by some to have been one Guglielmo Bevilacqua. Two massive pilons with towers support the bridge's three large arches, of which the widest measures 160 feet. An extremely picturesque effect is obtained by the use of red bricks, which also cover the swallow-tail battlements, creating a delicate contrast with the strips of white stone. At the beginning of the 19th century, the bridge's battlements were removed, but they were later replaced by Francis I of Austria. During the last war, much of the bridge was destroyed, but it was carefully reconstructed using the pieces recovered from the river bed. There are splendid panoramic views of the river and the city from the bridge, which is rightly considered one of the finest of early architectural works.

San Zeno

The church of San Zeno stands in an excellent position at the end of a huge square, giving it added prominence, alongside its Romanesque bell-tower (begun in 1045 and completed in 1149) and the splendid 13th-century tower of the Abbey. It stands on the site of various previous constructions dating from the 4th, 5th and 11th centuries, but the church as it appears today was begun in about 1120. Various extensions of the building were carried out throughout the 14th century, until it was completed in 1368, apart from the Gothic reconstruction of the apse and ceiling in 1398. In the lawn between the church and the bell-tower can still be seen today a sarcophagus which according to legend is the tomb of the famous medieval French king Pippin, and although there is no proof of this claim, nevertheless an age-old atmosphere of mystery seems to emanate from the Romanesque forms of the church. The façade clearly recalls the Cathedral of Modena in the small horizontal loggia motif, in the graceful porch, and in the slender pilaster strips, pillars and cornices. However, the strongly plastic emphasis of the Modenese church is lightened here by the warm colour of the Veronese stone, by the softer way in which the material is used, and by the luminous quality of the whole surface which is thus produced. Unified in conception and harmonious in design, the church has been attributed to Maestro Brioloto (active between 1189 and 1220), who certainly sculpted the rose-window's "Wheel of Fortune", linked to the porch below by narrow pilaster strips, while at the beginning of the 13th century an artist called Adamino da San Giorgio carved the *figures of animals* and *hunting scenes* along the cornices of the sloping roofs.

The statue of St. Zeno by an unknown sculptor of the 14th century and the Rose window, known as the "Wheel of Fortune", by Master Brioloto.

Previous page:
the façade of San Zeno.

San Zeno

Portal

The fine portal of the church was erected by one Maestro Nicolò in about 1138, after the dismantling of the previous portal. Over the doorway is an elegant porch, with two columns resting on *stylised lions* and supporting the baldachin. On the architraves, an unknown artist sculpted the series of the *Months*, while in the lunette above the door there is a basrelief depicting *St. Zeno among the foot soldiers and cavalry of the free city of Verona*. But the real masterpiece is constituted by the wooden doors themselves with their celebrated *bronze panels*. There are twenty-four on each door, with *scenes from the Bible, miracles of St. Zeno* and various symbolic and allegorical figures. They can be dated around the first years of the 1 2th century, and continue to represent a problem for critics as far as their stylistic and chronological collocation is concerned. They certainly contain echoes of the Ottonian doors on the Cathedral of Hildesheim, dating from the 11th century, but their artistic language is noticeably more vigorous and expressive. The scenes are not in logical order, and the heads of the figures project emphatically from the panels, while the action depicted seems almost to have been stopped and conveyed to us in the most immediate possible manner.

The bronze doors of San Zeno.

Right:
Christ in Glory and St. Zeno and the messengers from Gallien (details from the doors of San Zeno.)

Next page from the top:
Adam and Eve expelled from Paradise and the Beheading of St. John (details from the doors of San Zeno).

Bottom:
the First Labours, Cain and Abel and the Descent into Limbo (details from the doors of San Zeno).

The majestic interior
of San Zeno.

Next page:
the Crypt of San Zeno.

Interior

Divided into three naves, with raised chancel above the crypt, it has robust cruciform pillars alternating with slender columns, while a large transverse central arch interrupts the rhythmic progression of the round arches towards the apse. The Gothic wooden ceiling is an outstanding feature. There are 13th and 14th-century frescoes, which critics have attributed to unidentified first and second "Masters of San Zeno", and various works of Roman sculpture, including a porphyry bowl which legend has it was brought here by the devil, though it probably came from some Roman baths. In the chancel is a polychrome marble statue dear to the Veronese, depicting *San Zeno* and sculpted by an unknown master of the early 14th century.

The Virgin Mary,
central section of the
Mantegna Altarpiece.

Mantegna: altar-piece

This painting, the most precious masterpiece in the church, stands in all its splendour above the main altar. It is a triptych, painted by Andrea Mantegna between 1457 and 1459, clearly under the influence of the style of Donatello. The predella of the triptych was removed by the French and taken to the Louvre in Paris and the predella in San Zeno is a copy. Sculptural and architectural motifs are admirably combined in this work, and are united by the brilliant colour which is its dominant feature.

San Giovanni in Fonte

San Giovanni in Fonte was the original baptistry of the Cathedral, and its oldest parts date back to the 8th and 9th centuries, while the structure which can be seen today, with three naves and three apses, dates from 1123. The masterpiece in this small building is the *baptismal font*, one of the most important works of medieval sculpture in Verona, sculpted in about 1200. Octagonal in form, it has eight bas-relief panels sculpted on the outside of the basin, depicting *scenes from the life of Christ*, six of which are considered to be similar in style to the sculptures by Brioloto on the church of San Zeno, while the other two, the *Visitation* and the *Nativity*, seem to be by another artist.

One of the panels on the Baptismal Font and the interior of San Giovanni in Fonte.

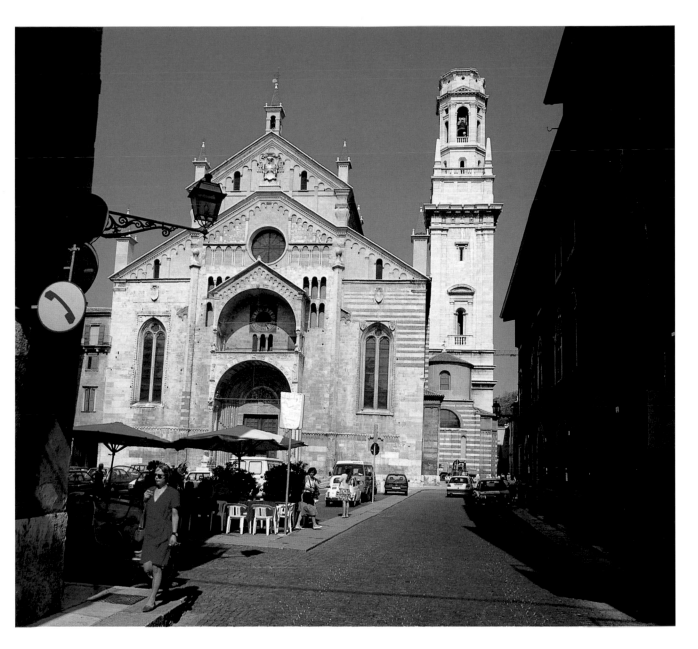

Cathedral

In a small square, which complements it to calculated effect, is Santa Maria Matricolare, the Cathedral of Verona. Built on the site of a previous Early Christian church and consecrated in 1187, the Cathedral has a façade which is a perfect composite of Romanesque and Gothic forms. The grandiose *porch*, consisting of a double baldachin supported by columns resting on *stylised lion figures*, is particularly striking. The portal is the work of Nicolò, the same artist who was responsible for the porch of San Zeno; here he sculpted various figures, including *prophets* and *animals*, the *legendary heroes* dear to the Middle Ages and *Biblical figures*. At the sides of the porch, two large Gothic windows are cut into the façade, while above it are three rows of miniature arcades, producing a chiaroscuro of light and shade. Higher up on the façade are spires and pinnacles which create an ever lighter effect towards the top. The bell-tower, the lower part of which is Romanesque, betrays the hand of Sanmicheli in the central section, while the upper part was completed by Fagiuoli in 1926. The interior is divided into three naves, with composite pillars of red marble supporting the ponderous arcades from which the cruciform vaults diverge. The church contains numerous works of art, among them the splendid *tomb of St. Agatha,* created by an unknown master in 1353.

The portal by Master Nicolò.

Previous page: the façade of the Cathedral (Duomo).

Duomo

Titian: The Assumption

Above the altar in the Nichesola Chapel, the first chapel in the left-hand nave, is the only work painted by Titian in Verona, the "Assumption", which he did between 1535 and 1540. One may compare this work with his other painting of the some subject in the Venetian church of Santa Maria Gloriosa dei Frari. Whereas in the latter the separation between the Virgin and the Apostles is much more marked, this altar-piece in Verona shows us a Madonna still of this world, more human perhaps in her attitude towards the reverent disciples.

Cloister

All that remains of the Early Christian church which stood on this site before the Cathedral are fragments of the mosaics from the floor, which can be seen here and there in the grass in the cloister. The cloister is a Romanesque structure dating from about 1140 and has arches supported by slender twin columns of red marble. Mention should also be made of the famous **Biblioteca Capitolare** nearby, a Library founded in the 5th century and thus one of the oldest in the world. It has an extremely rich collection of old books, as well as rare illuminated manuscripts, which make it one of the most precious deposits of Verona's cultural patrimony.

Partial view of the Cloister.

Previous page:
Altar-piece depicting
the Assumption by Titian.

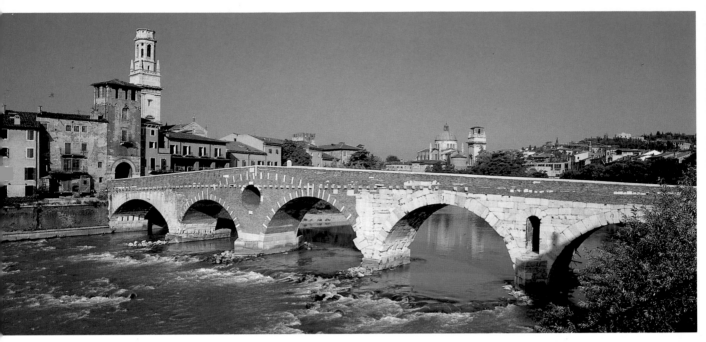

Ponte Pietra
(Stone Bridge).

Below:
Roman Herm
(Archaeological Museum).

Next page:
view of the Ponte Pietra
from the Roman Theatre.

Ponte Pietra

Verona had two bridges during the Roman era, the "pons postumius" and the "pons marmoreus". The first was completely destroyed by floods of the Adige during the 6th century, but the second, known as the Ponte Pietra, or "stone bridge", has remained largely intact. Constructed before the rule of Augustus, it has five arches of which the two closest to the left bank are Roman, while the two central arches were reconstructed during the 16th century.

The arch closest to the right bank was reconstructed in 1298 by Alberto I della Scala, together with the tall watchtower.

Here too the colours, the red of the bricks against the white of the stone, constitute the predominant note, creating an extremely picturesque effect with their reflections in the waters below.

Roman Theatre
Archeological Museum

Once more, as in so many other parts of this fable-like city, architecture and landscape combine to picturesque effect in the Roman Theatre, built in the Augustan age from

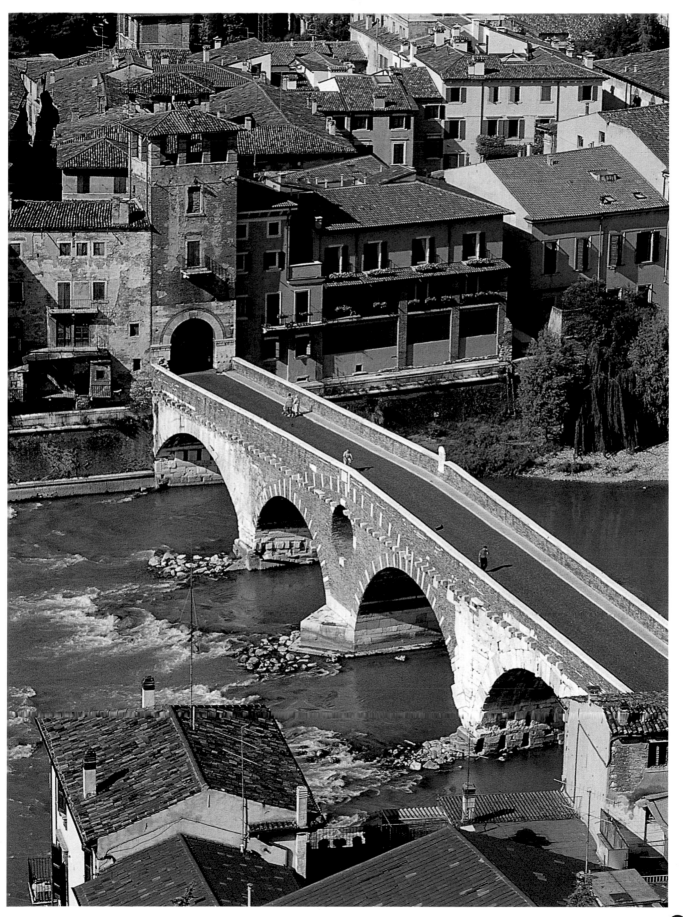

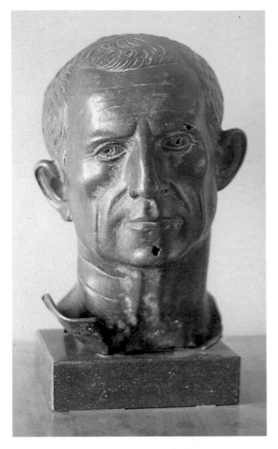

Archaeological Museum:
Bronze head of the
Augustan period and the
cloister of the Museum.

Below:
a room in the Museum.

stone which was later substituted by marble. The theatre now measures 360 feet by 455 feet, but it must have been much larger in its original state. Still intact are the semicircular seats, the stage and the two "wings", while the front of the theatre, the part facing the river which flows past under the ruins, has been lost.

Above the theatre is the imposing stone wall on which stands the ancient **Monastery of** **St. Jerome**, now the site of the **Archaeological Museum**.

The Museum has been recently rearranged and should definitely be visited by anyone interested in Roman Verona.

Sculpture, mosaics, bronze statuettes, glass, etc. are displayed inside the erstwhile monastery, whereas Roman sarcophagi and Veronese funeral monuments have been arranged around the courtyard and cloisters.

The entrance to the Roman Theatre and the tiers of the Theatre with a view of the Church of Saints Sirus and Libera.

Left:
view of Castel San Pietro.

Castel San Pietro

Climbing up to Castel San Pietro, one can see the ruins of the castle built by the Milanese rulers, the Visconti, during the brief period in which they governed Verona. The French began the demolition of the castle, and it was further demolished in 1854 by the Austrians when they built on top of the ruins a fortress whose splendid strategic position made it virtually impregnable. But more striking than the castle itself is the panoramic view which can be obtained from here. As one climbs up the hill to the castle, the city of Verona unfolds below: the river, the muted colours of the houses, the red roofs and the white Gothic spires, dominated by the tall bell-towers. Turning towards the right, one can see the pleasant hills behind the city and further away the mountains around Lake Garda.

The portal and the façade of Sant'Anastasia.

Sant' Anastasia

The largest church in Verona, it was begun in 1290 and not completed until the fast years of the 15th century. There was formerly a small church dedicated to Sant'Anastasia on the site and the name has survived, though this church was supposed to have been called San Pietro Martire, as it was built in honour of St. Peter Martyr, revered by the Dominicans. The façade remained unfinished, though clearly the designer intended it to be a grandiose structure, as can be seen from the lower part with its abundant use of colour and of plastic and architectural motifs. There are actually two doors within the deeply splayed Gothic arch of the portal, separated by a slim pillar, overlaid in turn by a small spiral column.

The frescoes in the lunettes can be dated at around the first years of the 15th century, but unfortunately today they are in very bad state. The right-hand pillar has bas-reliefs with *stories of St. Peter Martyr*, while there are other bas-reliefs on the entablature.

Apse

Like the façade and the interior of the church, the apse too gives an impression of grandeur. The splendid bell-tower is tall and slender, decorated with slim pilaster strips and small arch motifs.

Interior

The splendid interior is divided into three naves by twelve tall columns in red marble. The floor, typical with its red, white and blue inlays, is by Pietro da Forlezza and dates from 1462, while the vault has pictorial decoration with stylised flower motifs. In front of each of the first two pillars are two *holy-water stoups* supported by human figures, the famous "hunchbacks", images which seem almost somewhat bitter or ironic in the mystic atmosphere of the church. In Sant'Anastasia there are works by great artists such as Stefano da Verona, Lorenzo Veneziano, Michele Giambono, Girolamo dei Libri, Caroto and Morone. In the left-hand nave is the **Chapel of the Rosary**, containing the 14th-century panel of the *Madonna of the Rosary*.

Altichiero: votive fresco

This fresco by Altichiero, in the **Cavalli Chapel**, the first chapel on the right in the transept, can be dated at around 1390. The fresco depicts three knights belonging to the Cavalli family who, through the intercession of Saints George, Martin and James, ask for mercy from the Virgin, enthroned with the Christ Child.

The holy-water stoups in Sant'Anastasia, known as the "Hunchbacks".

The apse of
Sant'Anastasia.

Next page:
The church interior.

Page 54:
St. George and the
Princess (detail) by
Pisanello.

The scene takes place in an imaginary Gothic structure, full of arches, loggias and spires. Altichiero, the greatest northern Italian painter of the 14th century, derives his style from the great originator Giotto, though he translates Giotto's vision into gentler, more human terms, eliminating the sense of ineluctable cosmic grief which was the predominant note in Giotto.

Pisanello: St. George and the Princess

This fresco, painted for the Pellegrini Chapel, is now in the sacristy, following its recent restoration. It was painted between 1433 and 1438 by Pisanello, the most important representative of the so-called "International Gothic" style in northern Italy. In fact, the whole scene is full of the favourite motifs of the courtly Gothic painters – fantastic and imaginary landscapes (such as the Gothic city in the background), described with the minute skill of a calligrapher, peopled with purely symbolic figures (such as the two hanged men on the left). At the same time, Pisanello has depicted the action in its most essential moment, as the saint prepares to mount his horse and depart on his mission, under the fixed, aristocratic gaze of the Princess of Trebisond, whose profile stands out against the heavy drapery of her ermine cloak.

Porta dei Leoni
(Lion Gate).

Porta dei Leoni

This city gate, like the Arena, the Theatre and the Gavi Arch, is one of the most interesting remains of Roman Verona. Dating from the 1st century A. D., it originally consisted, before its later transformation, of two barrel vaults with columns at the sides and a tympanum. Above this was a series of arched windows and above the windows again an exedra. As with other Roman structures, the perfectly calculated dimensions of this monument did not fail to inspire the great artists of the Renaissance, who found abundant material in Verona for their works. Recent archaeological excavations in the area of the Gate have revealed its foundations as well as extensive sections of the road paving and the base of an ancient Roman tower. Everything is clearly visible in the specially constructed protective enclosure in the middle of the road flanking the Gate.

Recent archaeological excavations near Porta dei Leoni and Juliet's Tomb.

Juliet's Tomb

In a crypt in the cloister of a Capuchin monastery is the 13th-century sarcophagus of red marble which, so tradition has it, was the tomb of the tragic heroine Juliet. Naturally the legend is not supported by historical evidence, but those who have read the celebrated Shakespearean tragedy or who know the sad story of the young lovers are ready to believe that the mortal remains of Juliet once rested here. Apart from the cloister, the Baroque chapel of San Francesco can also be seen in the monastery, while nearby there is a display of frescoes detached from the walls of other Veronese churches, sufficiently representative to give a clear idea of the city's various artistic movements.

San Fermo Maggiore

On the site where Saints Fermus and Rusticus were martyred in 361, the Benedictine monks decided to build a vast church, consisting of two separate buildings, one above the other. The church was completed between 1065 and 1138, apart from later extensions and modifications.

The façade is thus an original mixture of Romanesque and Gothic forms: a deeply splayed portal, tall windows and horizontal bands in alternating colours.

But the most impressive part of the whole church is without doubt the apse: here the main apse, in Gothic style, is flanked by two minor apses which are Romanesque in tendency, while the red of the bricks contrasts effectively with the white, lacelike Gothic decorations, the tall pinnacles and the slender windows.

Above:
the façade and apse of
San Fermo Maggiore.

Left:
the church interior.

Page 58:
14th-century pulpit with
frescoes by Martino da
Verona and detail
of the Lower Church of
San Fermo Maggiore.

Giusti Gardens

Two views of the Giusti Gardens, splendid example of late Renaissance Italian gardens.

Begun in about 1580, this is considered one of the most beautiful of Italian gardens. It belongs to the Palazzo Giusti and is divided into two parts, a lower section in the Italian style, with a labyrinth, fountains and statues, and another section which extends up the hill of San Zeno in Monte. Here there is a long row of cypresses which have attracted many artists and writers, among them Goethe who, in 1786, is said to have actually carried away with him some branches of the trees.

The façade of the Saints Nazaro and Celso church and its external portal.

Below:
Santo Stefano church along the River Adige.

Saints Nazaro and Celso

The church is preceded by a great gateway (1688), the columns of which are curiously decorated with carved drapes. The elegant courtyard paved with geometrical designs leads up to the brick façade with its pointed arched porch and great Renaissance windows.

Built in the XVth Cent., the tri-part interior is flanked by side-chapels. **The Chapel of St. Blaise** (Cappella di San Biagio), a masterpiece by Beltramo di Valsolda (1488) is in the left transept, with a superb altar containing the *tomb of Saints Blaise and Juliana* by B. Panteo (1508). See also works by Girolamo dai Libri, Morone, Brusasorci, etc.

Santo Stefano

The church enjoys a splendid position on the left bank of the Adige next to the Roman Theatre. Tradition claims Santo Stefano as the first cathedral of Verona. Built above a former VIth Cent. oratory, it has a traditional, parti-coloured tufa and brick striped, hut-shaped façade with a porch

over the portal. The interior has a nave and two side-aisles, with a distinctive Romanesque ambulatory in the apse, where capitals from an earlier period have been readapted to the later structure.

The **Chapel of the Innocents** with Ottino frescoes (XVIIth Cent.), as well as works by Bassetti, Orbetto and others, deserves special attention.

San Giovanni in Valle

The church, with its pure, Romanesque linee, was founded in 1120 and was, for a certain period, the baptistery of the Cathedral. The façade, with its little hanging arches and frescoed porch, is flanked on the right by two wings of the ancient cloister.

The lower section of the Romanesque belltower is square. The tri-part interior is very evocative with its alternating columns and square pillare.

San Bernardino

The church is preceded by a spacious cloister and its brick façade is enhanced

by a fine Renaissance doorway. Founded in 1451, the single naved church is airy and full of light. Sanmicheli's **Pellegrini Chapel** is a Renaissance architectural masterpiece.

San Giorgio in Braida

The most important Renaissance church in Verona. The dome and the belltower were designed by Sanmicheli in the second half of the XVIth Cent. See works by Brusasorci, Veronese, Moretto and others.

Porta Palio and Porta Vescovo (Bishop's Gate), Porta San Zeno and Porta Nuova (New Gate).

The gates of Verona

Leaving aside the Lion Gate and the Porta Borsari which belonged to the ancient Roman walls, the other gateways were built in the XVIth Cent., when the Venetians strengthened Verona's defences, entrusting Michele Sanmicheli with the awesome military architectural task.

Porta Palio is perhaps the most classical of the doors designed by Sanmicheli and was part of the fortifications built to defend the town; it has three archways on its outer side and Doric semi-columns. It owes its name to the "Palio Race", which used to be run in the vicinity.

Porta Vescovo (Bishop's Gate) (XVth Cent.), is on the eastern side of the town. The turrets and the other parts of the superstructure were added under the Austrian domination during the last century.

Porta San Zeno (1541), was built in brick and topped with stone coats-of-arms and a pleasing serrated decorative motif.

Porta Nuova (New Gate). The main point of access into the town today, leading directly into Piazza Bra. The central section is by Sanmicheli (1535) and was later enlarged by adding two side-arches in 1854, during the Austrian domination.

Sanctuary of the Madonna of Lourdes

The Sanctuary of the Madonna of Lourdes rises to dominate Verona from the San Leonardo hill which encircles the Valdonega valley: the edifice sprang up in its two present forms starting in 1958 owing to events that make it one of the most significant places in the contemporary ecclesiastical history of the whole city. According to popular tradition, the whole zone of the Valdonega was dedicated by the Crusaders, on their return from the Holy Land, to the construction of a series of oratories, because of the resemblance of some of its landscapes with places in Palestine. Thus, one church was dedicated to St Mary of Nazareth, a second one to St Mary in Bethlehem, and a third one was called Holy Cross, in reference to the hill of Calvary at Jerusalem. On the San Leonardo hill, instead, from at least 1265 there rose a church dedicated to the Saint that had an adjoining monastery, the complex of which was to grow enormously before the dreadful earthquake that struck Verona in 1511. Today, only the Romanesque bell-tower, a part of the cloister and the apse of the church remain. In 1785, however, the monastery was de-consecrated until, thanks to its strategic position, the hill was designated by the Grand Duke, Maximilian of Hapsburg, as the seat of a military fortress, that was realised in 1838. Finally after the war, the complex, that had been used as a political prison between 1943 and 1945, was assigned to the Fathers of the Stigmatas for them to make it their new sanctuary. Having reached Verona shortly after their foundation (1853), the Fathers had first settled in Piazza Cittadella in what was called the Church of the Stigmatas; subsequently, owing to an increase in the religious family, they went to the church of St. Theresa which was re-consecrated to the Madonna of Lourdes and for which the sculptor Ugo Zannoni sculpted (1908) a *statue of the Virgin*, which was placed in a special grotto. During the Allied bombardments that hit Verona in 1945, the Church of the Stigmatas was destroyed, but the statue of the Madonna remained miraculously undamaged. In search

The Sanctuary of the Madona of Lourdes on San Leonardo Hill seen from the Adige and the statue of the Madonna of Lourdes.

of a new seat, the monks were assigned the old fortress of the San Leonardo hill; building of the present Sanctuary was begun in 1958 to the design of architect Paolo Rossi, over the structures of the ancient fort and with the adoption of a large body with a circular plan and protruding wings, realised with the most modern technologies involving the use of concrete. The statue of the Madonna was lodged in a modern new grotto on a terrace, so as to create in this way two places for worship: the actual church and the space outside the grotto open over the city.

Index